PATRICK LABERT

MONETIZE YOUR TALENT: WINNING CROWDFUNDING STRATEGIES FOR BLOGS, PODCASTS, YOUTUBE, AND PATREON

PATRICK LABERT

CONTENTS

PREFACE

In a constantly evolving world, where creativity and digital innovation intertwine with our daily lives, the power to turn passion into a profession is more accessible than ever. "Monetize Your Talent: Winning Crowdfunding Strategies for Blogs, Podcasts, YouTube, and Patreon" stems from the vision of exploring this dynamic landscape, providing digital content creators - from bloggers to podcasters, YouTubers to Patreon artists - with a compass to navigate the crowdfunding sea.

In this book, you will discover not only the 'how' but also the 'why' of crowdfunding. It's a journey that begins with understanding the foundations of this powerful financing tool, traversing the different landscapes of digital platforms, and culminating in the creation of a successful crowdfunding campaign.

I have written this book with both beginners and experts in mind, aiming to provide precise and in-depth information in clear and accessible language. You will find a balance between theory and practice, with concrete examples and case studies illuminating the path to follow. My desire is that each chapter not only offers you knowledge but also inspires you to take action, experiment, and dream big.

The world of crowdfunding is as diverse as the talents it seeks to support. Whether you're planning to launch your first podcast, expand your YouTube channel, enrich your blog, or make the most of Patreon, you will find the tools and strategies to do so successfully here.

In these pages, I have tried to infuse a sense of elegance and professionalism, befitting a book that speaks of self-realization and creative success. The stories, anecdotes, and advice contained in this book are meant to be not only informative but also a source of inspiration and motivation.

At the end of each chapter, I invite you to reflect, put into practice what you have learned, and make the discussed strategies your own. Fashion, after all, is not just what we see; it's an expression of who we are, our aspirations, and our commitment to excellence.

Welcome to an adventure that could not only change how you see crowdfunding but also how you view your talent and potential. Let's begin this journey together.

INTRODUCTION TO CROWDFUNDING

In the digital era, crowdfunding emerges as a silent revolution, a bridge between the world of ideas and the reality of the market. This chapter offers an exploratory journey into the heart of crowdfunding, a phenomenon that is reshaping the landscape of collective financing and democratizing access to capital.

Crowdfunding, or collective financing, is a practice that allows individuals to support ideas and projects through small financial contributions, often collected online. This mechanism opens the doors to a multitude of possibilities, making funding accessible for projects that would otherwise remain unexplored.

The history of crowdfunding takes us back in time, showing how a simple idea gave birth to a global movement. From fundraising for artistic projects to platforms that support a variety of initiatives, crowdfunding has evolved into a fundamental tool for artists, entrepreneurs, and innovators.

There are various forms of crowdfunding, each with its characteristics and peculiarities. From donation-based crowdfunding, where support is offered without expectations of material return, to reward-based crowdfunding, where supporters receive a product or service in exchange for their contribution. Other forms include equity-based crowdfunding, which offers a stake in the company, and lending crowdfunding, similar to a loan with interest.

In addition to fundraising, crowdfunding serves as a

powerful marketing and market validation tool. It allows creators to test the public's interest in their ideas, receiving not only funding but also valuable feedback and an initial supporter base.

Understanding the psychology of supporters is crucial. The reasons people contribute to a project vary, from the desire to be part of something bigger to supporting causes or ideas they deeply believe in.

Online crowdfunding platforms like Kickstarter, Indiegogo, and Patreon play a central role in this ecosystem. They provide the necessary structure to launch and promote campaigns, offering visibility and accessibility to a vast global audience.

Creating a successful crowdfunding campaign requires more than just a good idea. It demands a compelling narrative, a solid marketing strategy, realistic goals, and complete transparency. This segment explores the key steps to create an effective and engaging campaign.

Despite its great potential, crowdfunding presents challenges. Market saturation, project failure risk, and ethical issues are aspects that require attention and a careful approach.

Concluding this introduction with an analysis of case studies in the crowdfunding world, insights and practical lessons are offered, showing how different strategies can lead to very different results.

This overview of crowdfunding is designed to provide a comprehensive understanding of this versatile tool, laying the groundwork for a deeper exploration of its applications in the world of blogs, podcasts, YouTube channels, and Patreon. This journey promises to be rich in information, inspiration, and practical applications.

DEFINITION AND OVERVIEW

Crowdfunding, at its core, represents a revolution in project and idea financing. It is a method that allows individuals, groups, or companies to raise funds to bring an idea or project to life by appealing not only to a single investor or institution but to a broad community of people, often through online platforms. This practice has opened new horizons in funding creative, entrepreneurial, social, and technological initiatives.

The underlying idea of crowdfunding is relatively simple yet profoundly revolutionary: instead of relying on a few investors providing large sums of money, it leverages a multitude of individuals contributing smaller amounts. This democratization of financing not only makes it possible to realize projects that would otherwise remain unrealized but also provides creators with a direct and immediate way to gauge the public's interest in their ideas.

With the rise of the internet and the expansion of social media, crowdfunding has become more accessible and widespread. Online crowdfunding platforms specializing in this process serve as crucial intermediaries, providing tools and infrastructure that allow creators to present their ideas to an international audience, set fundraising goals, and receive funding. These platforms vary in focus, with some concentrating on creative and artistic projects, others on entrepreneurial initiatives or social causes.

In addition to being a means of raising capital, crowdfunding also serves as a marketing and market validation tool.

Successful campaigns not only reach or exceed fundraising goals but also build a base of enthusiastic and engaged supporters, creating a community around a project or idea. This aspect is particularly valuable as it provides creators with immediate feedback and market insights, as well as a platform for launching and promoting their work.

For creators and entrepreneurs, crowdfunding represents a unique opportunity to obtain funding without the traditional constraints and restrictions imposed by conventional funding avenues. This freedom allows for greater flexibility and creativity, enabling them to explore innovative and sometimes risky ideas that might not otherwise be funded.

In a world where innovation and creativity are increasingly in the spotlight, crowdfunding emerges as a fundamental tool. It's not just about raising funds; it's a movement that empowers people to realize their visions, breaking down traditional barriers and making the path from idea to success more accessible and inclusive.

RELEVANCE OF CROWDFUNDING FOR DIGITAL CREATORS

Crowdfunding has become of paramount importance for digital creators, offering them a vital platform to launch and promote their projects. This method of collective financing aligns perfectly with the digital context, which is inherently characterized by creativity, innovation, and a constant need for renewal.

In the crowdfunding ecosystem, content creators such as filmmakers, game developers, musicians, and podcasters find fertile ground. Crowdfunding platforms reduce traditional barriers to accessing capital, allowing these creatives to present their ideas directly to an international audience. This direct and democratized access to funding is revolutionary, especially for those working with limited resources and seeking to test their ideas in the market without significant initial investment.

Building and engaging with the community are crucial aspects of crowdfunding. When people decide to fund a project, they often develop a sense of ownership and active participation in its development. This direct connection between creators and supporters is invaluable, as it provides creators with immediate feedback and valuable insights into their audience's expectations.

In addition to being an effective means of raising funds, crowdfunding also serves as a powerful market validation tool. A successful crowdfunding campaign not only raises the necessary capital to realize a project but also demonstrates that there is genuine interest in the proposed idea or product. This form of validation is fundamental in the digital context where understanding and capturing the audience's attention are crucial.

Another significant aspect of crowdfunding is the flexibility and creative freedom it offers to creators. Unlike traditional funding methods, which may impose compromises or restrictions, crowdfunding allows creatives to stay true to their original vision. This autonomy is precious in the digital world, where uniqueness and authenticity are often the keys to success.

However, crowdfunding is not without its challenges. Creating and managing a campaign requires a significant commitment in terms of time, energy, and resources. Creators must be able to effectively communicate their vision, produce compelling marketing materials, and manage the expectations of their supporters. Despite these challenges, for those who can successfully navigate this environment, crowdfunding offers an unprecedented opportunity to bring innovative ideas to the market, build a base of loyal supporters, and pave the way for future creative initiatives.

In summary, crowdfunding is not just a means of raising capital; it is an innovation accelerator and a bridge between creative ideas and their practical realization. For digital creators, it represents a path to bring their visions to life, engage the audience, and leave an indelible mark in the digital landscape.

PART I: FUNDAMENTALS OF CROWDFUNDING

Crowdfunding, a revolution in the world of financing, has become a fundamental pillar for numerous projects and initiatives across various sectors. This first part of the book is dedicated to exploring the fundamental principles of crowdfunding, providing a solid knowledge base from which digital creators can draw to turn their visions into tangible realities.

We begin with an in-depth examination of what crowdfunding actually is. This concept, which literally means "funding from the crowd," is based on the idea of gathering small amounts of money from a large number of people, typically through the Internet. This approach democratizes project funding, making it accessible to a wide variety of people and ideas.

Next, we delve into the history and evolution of crowdfunding. While the idea of raising funds from a large group of people is not new, the advent of the Internet has radically transformed this practice. Online platforms have opened new avenues for fundraising, allowing projects to reach a global audience and raise significant sums of money.

We then explore the different types of crowdfunding. These include donation-based crowdfunding, where supporters contribute without expecting anything in return; reward-based crowdfunding, which offers supporters products, services, or experiences in exchange for their support; equity-based crowdfunding, which allows investors to purchase ownership shares in a company; and lending-based crowdfunding, where contributions are treated as loans to be repaid with interest. Each type has its peculiarities and suits different types of projects and goals.

The chapter continues with a discussion of how and why crowdfunding attracts both creators and supporters. For creators, crowdfunding is not just a way to raise funds but also a platform to validate their ideas and build a community of supporters. For supporters, contributing to a crowdfunding campaign often means having the opportunity to be part of something bigger, directly supporting ideas and projects they believe in.

We also examine the psychology behind crowdfunding, seeking to understand what motivates people to contribute to a project. This aspect is crucial for creating successful crowdfunding campaigns, as understanding supporters' motivations can help creators structure their campaigns more effectively.

Additionally, we discuss the crucial role of crowdfunding platforms. These websites not only facilitate fundraising but also offer essential tools for campaign management, communication with supporters, and project promotion. Choosing the right platform can have a significant impact on the success of a campaign.

Finally, we focus on how to create a successful crowdfunding campaign. This includes campaign planning, crafting a compelling message, setting realistic goals, and effectively promoting the campaign. Post-campaign management is also vital, as it ensures that supporters are kept informed and involved in the project realization process.

This first part of the book lays the foundation for a comprehensive understanding of crowdfunding, providing readers with the knowledge and tools necessary to navigate successfully in this exciting and dynamic field.

WHY CROWDFUNDING IS EFFECTIVE

Crowdfunding has proven to be an extremely effective method of financing projects and initiatives, especially in the digital sector. This effectiveness stems from a combination of unique factors that make it a valuable resource for both creators and supporters.

One of the most powerful aspects of crowdfunding is its ability to democratize funding. Unlike traditional channels, which are often limited by strict requirements and accessible only to a select elite, crowdfunding opens the door to a wide range of ideas and projects. Anyone with an internet connection can present their idea to a global audience, regardless of their geographic location or economic background. This openness removes many barriers, allowing a diverse array of projects to find the support they need.

The nature of crowdfunding also allows for direct market validation. When a project receives funding from the "crowd," it indicates genuine market interest. This not only provides creators with the funds needed to develop their project but also confirms that there is a demand for their product or service. In other words, the success of a crowdfunding campaign serves as an indicator that the project has an audience, thus reducing the associated investment risk.

Crowdfunding also fosters a strong sense of community and engagement. Supporters of a crowdfunding project often feel integral to the project's success. This sense of belonging not only motivates further contributions but can also lead to project promotion through word-of-mouth. Supporters become ambassadors for the project, spreading awareness within their personal and professional networks.

Another advantage of crowdfunding is its ability to provide flexibility and control to creators. Unlike traditional funding, which may involve relinquishing some control of the project to external investors, crowdfunding allows creators to maintain full creative and decision-making control. This is particularly important in fields such as art, music, film, and technology, where creative vision and originality are essential.

Furthermore, crowdfunding serves as a powerful marketing and communication tool. Crowdfunding campaigns often attract media attention, increasing the visibility of both the project and its creator. This exposure can be extremely valuable, leading to additional opportunities beyond the initial funding.

Finally, crowdfunding offers creators a unique opportunity for experimentation and innovation. In a context where traditional methods may discourage risky or unconventional projects, crowdfunding encourages the exploration of new and creative ideas. This opens the doors to projects that might otherwise never see the light of day, fostering diversity and innovation in the creative landscape.

In conclusion, the effectiveness of crowdfunding is based on a combination of accessibility, market validation, community engagement, creative control, media visibility, and encouragement of innovation. These factors together create an environment where ideas can flourish and transform into tangible realities, benefiting both creators and supporters.

BENEFITS FOR BLOGS, PODCASTS, AND YOUTUBE CHANNELS

Crowdfunding has emerged as an effective and versatile method of funding, particularly suitable for digital content creators such as bloggers, podcasters, and YouTubers. These benefits are manifold and touch various aspects of content production, community growth, and economic support.

For bloggers, crowdfunding offers a direct way to monetize their work and fund more ambitious projects. In an environment where generating revenue can be challenging, especially in the early stages, crowdfunding provides bloggers with the freedom to create high-quality content without relying solely on advertising or sponsorships. This can lead to greater editorial independence and a more authentic connection with their audience.

In the world of podcasting, crowdfunding is essential for covering production costs, which can include equipment, editing, hosting, and, in some cases, even compensation for guests or the production team. Through crowdfunding, podcasters can also experiment with riskier or niche formats and topics, knowing they have the support of a community that appreciates their work.

For YouTube content creators, crowdfunding represents an alternative or complementary source of funding to advertising revenue. This is particularly important in a context where monetization policies can be uncertain and variable. Crowdfunding allows YouTubers to undertake larger or higher-quality projects, such as more elaborate series, documentaries, or educational content, which would otherwise be difficult to produce solely with advertising income.

Another significant advantage of crowdfunding for all these creators is the ability to build and strengthen a community of supporters. The success of a crowdfunding campaign is measured not only in economic terms but also in the enthusiasm and engagement of the audience. This community not only supports the project financially but also becomes a source of feedback, ideas, and encouragement, creating a virtuous cycle of interaction and growth.

Furthermore, crowdfunding enables creators to test new ideas and receive valid confirmation of their interest from the audience. This immediate feedback is crucial for developing content that truly responds to the needs and interests of their audience.

Finally, crowdfunding offers digital creators greater autonomy and creative control. By breaking free from dependence on traditional funding sources, creators can remain true to their original vision and explore themes they deem important without having to compromise to cater to the interests of sponsors or advertisers.

In summary, crowdfunding opens up new possibilities for digital content creators, providing them with tools to finance their projects, strengthen their communities, test new ideas, and maintain a high degree of independence and creative integrity.

ACTIVE COMMUNITY ENGAGEMENT

Active community engagement in crowdfunding is a fundamental aspect that goes beyond simply funding a project. This interaction creates a unique bond between creators and their audience, bringing mutual benefits and fueling the success of the campaign.

Building an Engaged Community

In crowdfunding, the community is not just a passive audience; it becomes an active part of the creative process. Supporters invest not only money but also time, interest, and passion. This emotional investment creates a sense of belonging and ownership towards the project, encouraging the community to be more involved and active in their support.

Feedback and Collaborative Development

One of the major advantages of active community engagement is the opportunity to receive valuable feedback. Creators can leverage their base of supporters to test ideas, gather suggestions, and make improvements. In some cases, this can even evolve into a form of collaborative development, where the community contributes significantly to the direction and shape of the project.

Promotion and Advocacy

An actively engaged community becomes a powerful tool for

promotion. Enthusiastic supporters often share their excitement with friends, family, and colleagues, increasing the project's visibility. This organic word-of-mouth is incredibly effective because it is driven by genuine trust and credibility.

Retention and Long-Term Support

Community engagement through crowdfunding extends beyond the duration of the campaign. This participation can transform into long-term support, with supporters becoming loyal fans of the creator's work. This kind of lasting relationship is crucial for creators looking to build a sustainable career and have a lasting impact.

Emotional and Motivational Benefits

Interacting with a committed community can offer significant emotional benefits to creators. Seeing that their work is appreciated and directly supported by a community can be extremely motivating and gratifying. This moral support is often as valuable as financial support.

Challenges and Community Management

Managing active community engagement also presents challenges. Creators must strike the right balance between considering community feedback and maintaining their original vision. Additionally, transparent and regular communication is essential to maintain the trust and interest of the community.

Engagement in the Post-Funding Phase

Finally, community engagement does not end with reaching the funding goal. Creators often continue to involve their supporters in the development and realization phases of the project, keeping the community informed and engaged until the final launch of the product or service.

In conclusion, active community engagement in crowdfunding is a vital element that enriches the experience for both creators and supporters. This interaction not only increases the chances of a campaign's success but also builds a solid foundation for future relationships and ongoing support for creative projects.

TYPES OF CROWDFUNDING

Donation, Lending, Reward, Equity, Content Crowdfunding

Crowdfunding comes in various forms, each with specific characteristics and purposes. Understanding the differences between these types is crucial for creators and entrepreneurs to choose the approach that best suits their project.

Donation Crowdfunding: This type of crowdfunding is based on the principle of donations. Supporters financially contribute to the project without expecting anything in return. Donation crowdfunding is often used for social causes, charities, humanitarian aid, or artistic and cultural projects. In this model, emotional connection and trust in the project or cause are key factors that drive people to donate.

Lending Crowdfunding: Also known as lending-based crowdfunding, in this model, supporters lend money to the project or company with the promise of being repaid over time, often with interest. Lending crowdfunding is primarily used by small businesses or startups in need of capital to grow. This model is similar to a bank loan, but the funding comes from a multitude of investors rather than a single financial institution.

Reward Crowdfunding: In this variant, supporters receive a tangible reward or service in exchange for their financial contribution. Rewards can vary based on the donated amount and are often related to the product or project in question. This type of crowdfunding is highly popular among content creators, inventors, and entrepreneurs because it provides supporters with a concrete incentive, thus enhancing the campaign's appeal.

Equity Crowdfunding: In this model, supporters become investors by purchasing ownership shares in the company or project. Equity crowdfunding is often used by startups or small to medium-sized businesses seeking venture capital. Investors are motivated by the prospect of a financial return if the project or company succeeds, but they must also be aware of the risk of losing their investment if the project fails.

Content Crowdfunding: Specifically designed for content creators such as artists, musicians, writers, and YouTubers, content crowdfunding focuses on funding creative projects. In this model, supporters financially contribute to an individual or project in exchange for exclusive access to content, experiences, or interactions. Platforms like Patreon are examples of this type of crowdfunding, where fans can support their favorite creators with monthly subscriptions in exchange for exclusive content or personalized benefits.

Each type of crowdfunding has its own unique characteristics and is suitable for different situations and goals. Choosing the right model depends on the nature of the project, financial needs, the type of supporters you want to attract, and the long-term objectives of the creator or company.

SELECTING THE APPROPRIATE CROWDFUNDING MODEL

Choosing the right crowdfunding model is a crucial step that requires a clear understanding of the project's goals, target audience, and the nature of the initiative itself. Each type of crowdfunding has its own specificities and may be more or less suitable depending on the circumstances and needs of the project.

Before selecting the crowdfunding model, it is essential to clearly define the project's objective and what you intend to achieve with the funding. This helps in determining the most suitable model. For example, if the goal is to launch an innovative product in the market, reward crowdfunding might be the most suitable option as it allows you to offer the product itself as a reward to supporters. Conversely, if you are raising funds for a social or humanitarian cause, donation crowdfunding may be more appropriate as it is based on solidarity and the desire to support a good cause without expectations of material return.

Another aspect to consider is the target audience. Different types of crowdfunding attract different types of supporters. While lending and equity crowdfunding tend to attract investors interested in a financial return, reward and content crowdfunding are more suitable for projects that can create a strong emotional connection with the audience, such as artistic or creative initiatives.

Understanding your network of contacts and the ability to reach a broader audience is also essential. Some projects may have more immediate appeal within a specific community, which could influence the choice of crowdfunding model. For example, a project with strong local appeal may succeed with a community-based donation crowdfunding campaign, while a project with global potential may benefit from reward or content crowdfunding to reach a broader audience online.

Additionally, it's important to consider the level of commitment and resources available to manage the crowdfunding campaign. Different models require different levels of commitment in creating and managing the campaign, communicating with supporters, and delivering rewards or returns. For example, a reward crowdfunding campaign may require significant logistics for the production and distribution of rewards, while an equity crowdfunding campaign requires an understanding of the legal and financial implications of offering company shares.

Finally, evaluating the potential long-term impact of the chosen crowdfunding model on the project or business is crucial. While some models may offer a quick funding solution, others may have long-term implications, as in the case of equity crowdfunding, where a portion of the company's ownership is relinquished.

In summary, choosing the appropriate crowdfunding model requires careful analysis of objectives, target audience, available resources, and long-term implications. A well-considered decision at this stage can make the difference between the success or failure of a crowdfunding campaign.

PART II: CROWDFUNDING FOR CONTENT CREATORS

Part II of the book is specifically dedicated to crowdfunding for content creators, exploring how this method of financing can be effectively used by bloggers, podcasters, YouTubers, artists, and other digital creatives. This section aims to provide an in-depth guide for navigating the world of crowdfunding, showing how to turn creative passions into community-funded and supported projects.

We begin with a detailed analysis of the peculiarities of crowdfunding in the context of content creators. This segment explores how different crowdfunding platforms suit various types of creative projects, from blogs to videos, music to podcasts, and how these platforms can be used to reach a specific audience and engage the community in unique and creative ways.

Next, we focus on planning and developing a crowdfunding campaign for creative projects. This part includes defining campaign goals, choosing the most suitable crowdfunding model, and creating a compelling narrative that captures the audience's attention and interest. Practical tips will be provided on how to structure rewards, set realistic goals, and effectively use communication channels to promote the campaign.

We then address the theme of community management and maintenance during and after the campaign. This includes strategies to keep supporters engaged and interested, regular updates on project development, and tips on how to turn occasional supporters into long-term fans. The importance of honest feedback and transparent communication is emphasized as key to building a relationship of trust and mutual support with the community.

Another key topic in this section is the analysis of successful and failed case studies in crowdfunding for content creators. These concrete examples provide valuable insights into the factors contributing to a campaign's success, common pitfalls to avoid, and best practices to follow. These case studies also serve as a source of inspiration and motivation, showing what can be achieved through crowdfunding.

Finally, Part II discusses the challenges and future opportunities in crowdfunding for content creators. It explores how the crowdfunding landscape is evolving and what the new trends and emerging opportunities might be. This section aims to provide creators with a long-term vision and an understanding of potential developments in this field, allowing them to adapt and make the most of the opportunities that arise.

In summary, Part II of the book is a comprehensive resource that guides content creators through every aspect of crowdfunding, from campaign planning to post-campaign management. The goal is to provide the tools and knowledge needed to transform creative ideas into successfully realized projects, supported by a community of enthusiasts and supporters.

SPECIFIC STRATEGIES FOR DIFFERENT PLATFORMS

Specific crowdfunding strategies vary significantly depending on the platform used. Each platform has its unique characteristics and, consequently, requires a different approach. In this section, we will explore how to tailor crowdfunding strategies to maximize success on various platforms, such as blogs, podcasts, YouTube, and Patreon.

Strategies for Blogs: Bloggers can use crowdfunding to finance special projects, in-depth research, or series of articles. The key to success in this context is to create engaging storytelling that illustrates the value and uniqueness of the proposed content. Bloggers must clearly communicate how the funds raised will improve the quality and depth of their work. Offering exclusive rewards, such as access to premium content, private Q&A sessions, or special mentions in the blog, can incentivize readers to contribute.

Strategies for Podcasts: Podcasters can use crowdfunding to enhance the production quality, fund special episodes, or thematic series. It's essential for podcasters to leverage the personal connection they have with their audience by sharing personal stories and the passion behind their work. Offering rewards like early access to episodes, exclusive content, or the opportunity to participate in an episode can be particularly effective.

Strategies for YouTube: YouTubers often turn to crowdfunding to finance more ambitious video projects or purchase better equipment. In this case, visual demonstration of the project and its potential outcomes is crucial. Creating promotional videos that showcase what you intend to achieve can help convince potential supporters. Rewards such as shoutouts in videos, custom merchandise, or the chance to appear in a video can be very appealing to supporters.

Strategies for Patreon: Patreon is unique in the crowdfunding landscape as it is based on a model of ongoing support rather than a single campaign. Here, the focus is on building a long-term relationship with supporters. Creators must provide a steady stream of valuable content to keep their audience engaged. Offering subscription tiers with progressively more attractive benefits, such as access to exclusive chats, behind-the-scenes videos, or the ability to influence future content, can encourage continuous support.

In all these platforms, clear, authentic, and regular communication with the audience is crucial. Creators should explain how the funds will be used and show appreciation for every level of support. It is also important to keep the audience updated on the project's progress and any challenges encountered along the way.

In summary, each platform requires a tailored approach to crowdfunding, taking into account its specific dynamics and the type of audience it targets. By adapting the strategy to the context, content creators can maximize their chances of success in their crowdfunding campaigns.

UNIQUE APPROACHES FOR BLOGS, PODCASTS, AND YOUTUBE CHANNELS IN CROWDFUNDING

Unique Approaches for Crowdfunding in Blogs:

- Bloggers can leverage their storytelling skills to create a compelling narrative around their crowdfunding project. Sharing the origins of the blog, personal motivations behind writing, and future goals can create a strong emotional bond with readers.

- Offering exclusive content as rewards, such as access to special posts, e-books, or series previews, can be a strong incentive for the audience. This approach not only rewards supporters but also adds value to the contribution they are providing.

- Direct interaction with readers through comments, surveys, or live streaming can increase engagement. This allows supporters to feel more involved in the creative process and can encourage further donations.

Unique Approaches for Crowdfunding in Podcasts:

- Podcasters have a unique opportunity to create a personal connection through their medium. Sharing personal stories, challenges, and successes related to the podcast can make listeners more likely to financially support the project.

- Offering exclusive audio content, such as bonus episodes, Q&A sessions, or previews of new series, represents an effective form of reward for supporters. These additional contents can be made available only to those contributing to the crowdfunding.

- Giving listeners the opportunity to influence the future content of the podcast or to participate directly in some special episodes can be a powerful incentive for engagement and support.

Unique Approaches for Crowdfunding on YouTube Channels:

- YouTubers can leverage their visual format to effectively showcase what they intend to achieve with their crowdfunding project. Promotional videos that outline the plans and objectives of the project can help visualize the value and impact of the initiative.

- Engaging the audience through videos by offering personalized thank-yous, shoutouts in videos, or the opportunity to appear in a video can significantly increase interaction with the community. This approach can make supporters an integral part of the project.

- Providing regular and transparent updates on the project's development through videos helps maintain high interest among supporters. This allows for open and transparent communication with the community, strengthening trust and commitment to the project.

In each of these platforms, it is crucial for creators to maintain authentic and transparent communication with their supporters. Showing gratitude for every contribution and keeping the audience informed about the project's progress and challenges is essential for building a trusting relationship and sustaining long-term engagement with the community. By implementing these specific and personalized approaches, creators can optimize their crowdfunding campaigns and forge a deeper connection with their audience.

PATREON AS A VERSATILE MONETIZATION TOOL

Patreon has become an extremely versatile monetization tool for a wide range of content creators, from musicians and artists to bloggers and videomakers. This platform is based on a monthly subscription model, offering a unique and sustainable approach to funding creative projects.

Versatility and sustainability are among the key features of Patreon. Unlike other forms of crowdfunding that focus on single, short-term campaigns, Patreon allows creators to establish a regular and predictable income stream. This aspect is crucial for those looking to build a lasting and sustainable career in the creative field.

The platform stands out for the ability it gives creators to customize their subscription model. They can offer different levels of support, each with specific rewards, allowing supporters to choose the option that best suits their interests and financial capabilities. This customization promotes greater flexibility and enables creators to tailor their offering to the needs and desires of their audience.

Direct connection with supporters is another key aspect of Patreon. Creators can interact directly with their community, receiving feedback and suggestions that can guide the development of their content. This direct relationship not only strengthens the bond with supporters but also provides creators with valuable insights into what their audience truly desires.

Furthermore, Patreon provides creators with the freedom

and creative control over their projects. Without the pressure to conform to sponsor or advertiser requirements, creators can explore bolder and more original ideas while staying true to their artistic vision.

Finally, the platform can also serve as a marketing tool. By showcasing their projects and building a community on Patreon, creators increase the visibility of their work. This visibility can attract new supporters and open up additional opportunities for professional growth and development.

In conclusion, Patreon represents a dynamic and adaptable monetization solution that aligns well with the needs and goals of a wide variety of content creators, offering them an effective means to build a sustainable career in the digital world.

SETTING UP A SUCCESSFUL PATREON CAMPAIGN

To establish a successful campaign on Patreon, a strategic and well-thought-out approach is essential. Here are some key steps:

Clear Definition of Goals and Vision: Before launching a Patreon campaign, it's crucial to have a precise vision of what you want to achieve. Set concrete goals and understand how Patreon fits into your monetization and growth strategy.

Development of Engaging Content: The heart of a Patreon campaign is the content you offer. Create content that resonates with your audience and provides unique value. Exclusive content, early access, behind-the-scenes material, or personalized materials can make a difference.

Structuring Support Tiers and Rewards: Configure support tiers to offer various options for different supporters. Each tier should have clear and enticing rewards, and you should ensure that you can deliver what you promise. Balance rewards with feasibility to make sure you can fulfill your commitments.

Consistent and Authentic Communication: Maintaining open and regular communication with supporters is vital.

Update them on progress, share successes and challenges, and show appreciation for their support. This helps build a community around your work.

Active Campaign Promotion: Actively promote your Patreon campaign through various channels. This may include social media, links in your works, and collaborations with other creators to expand your reach. Engage your existing audience and encourage them to spread the word.

Listening and Adaptation: Be open to feedback and ready to adjust your Patreon strategy based on the needs and desires of your supporters. This may involve tweaking support tiers, modifying rewards, or changing the direction of your content.

Periodic Evaluation and Adjustments: Periodically assess the success of your campaign and make necessary changes to maintain supporter interest. Analyze metrics such as the number of supporters, retention rates, and feedback to guide your adjustments.

By following these steps, content creators can build a solid base of supporters on Patreon, which will help them realize their creative projects and build a sustainable career in the digital world.

UNIQUE FEATURES OF PATREON

Patreon stands out among crowdfunding platforms due to several unique features that make it particularly suitable for creators of various types of content. These features have been designed to address the specific needs of creators seeking continuous financial support and a deeper connection with their fan base.

Recurring Support Model: Unlike other crowdfunding platforms that focus on individual campaigns for specific projects, Patreon operates on a recurring support model. Creators receive regular contributions (usually monthly) from their supporters, providing a more stable and predictable source of income. This model is particularly useful for creators who produce content regularly.

Customizable Subscription Tiers: Patreon allows creators to set up different subscription levels, each with its own specific rewards. This gives creators the flexibility to offer various options to supporters, from credits in their work to access to exclusive content, and even more personalized experiences. This system helps cater to different segments of the audience, from occasional fans to dedicated supporters.

Direct Relationship with Supporters: The platform facilitates a direct and personal relationship between creators and their supporters. Creators can communicate directly with their fans through updates, exclusive posts, and direct interactions. This proximity helps build a stronger and more engaged community around the creator and their work.

Creative Flexibility and Independence: Patreon offers creators the freedom to explore and develop their projects without the pressure to conform to sponsor or publisher guidelines. Creators have complete control over the type of content they produce, allowing them to stay true to their artistic and creative vision.

Metrics and Analytics: The platform provides analytics tools to monitor campaign performance, supporter engagement, and income trends. These data can help creators optimize their content and promotion strategies to maximize support.

Community and Networking: Patreon is not just a crowdfunding platform but also a community of creators and enthusiasts. Creators have the opportunity to connect with other professionals in their field, share experiences, advice, and collaborate on joint projects.

In summary, the unique features of Patreon make it an ideal choice for content creators seeking sustainable financial support, a closer relationship with their audience, and the freedom to express their creativity without constraints.

CREATING AND CUSTOMIZING A PATREON CAMPAIGN

Creating and customizing a Patreon campaign requires a blend of creativity, strategic planning, and a personal touch. Here's a comprehensive guide on how to set up and personalize a Patreon campaign to maximize its impact and success.

Start with a Clear Vision: First and foremost, you need to have a clear vision of what you want to achieve with your Patreon campaign. What type of content are you planning to produce? What are your long-term goals? Understanding your artistic direction and objectives will help you effectively communicate the value of your work to potential supporters.

Choose the Right Subscription Model: Patreon offers the flexibility to create different subscription tiers, each with its unique rewards. These can range from credits in your work to exclusive content, access to special events, or virtual meetings. It's important to offer a variety of options to attract a broader range of supporters, keeping in mind that each subscription level should provide value proportionate to the contribution.

Create Compelling and Engaging Content: The heart of your Patreon campaign will be the content you offer. Whether it's videos, blog articles, artwork, music, or podcasts, your content should reflect your uniqueness and passion. Consider offering exclusive previews, behind-the-scenes looks, or creation processes to give your supporters a sense of exclusive involvement in your creative process.

Communication and Transparency: Open and honest communication is crucial for building and maintaining trust with your supporters. Provide regular updates on project status, share your inspirations, the challenges you encounter, and your successes. This not only keeps supporters informed but also strengthens the sense of community.

Engage with Supporters: Patreon offers a unique platform to interact directly with your fans. Use this opportunity to engage supporters in content creation, perhaps through voting on what to create next or Q&A sessions. This level of interaction can increase engagement and loyalty.

Utilize Marketing Tools: Promote your Patreon campaign through your existing channels—social media, website, newsletters—and consider collaborations with other creators to expand your reach. Tell the story behind your art and creative journey so that the audience can emotionally connect with your cause.

Monitor and Adapt: Use Patreon's analytical tools to monitor your campaign's performance. Pay attention to data such as sign-up and cancellation rates, and use this information to adapt your strategy. Being flexible and willing to adjust your offerings based on supporter feedback is essential for long-term success.

In conclusion, a successful Patreon campaign requires more than just quality content; it needs a well-thought-out strategy, effective communication, and an authentic connection with your supporter base. With the right combination of creativity, engagement, and transparency, you can turn your Patreon into a sustainable source of support and growth for your art.

PART III: BUILDING YOUR CAMPAIGN

Building a successful crowdfunding campaign is a crucial phase for content creators and requires careful and thorough planning. Part III of the book is dedicated to guiding you through this process, covering various fundamental aspects of creating an effective campaign.

Planning and Preparation: This phase includes defining the campaign's goals, choosing the most suitable crowdfunding platform, and studying strategies of similar campaigns to identify elements of success and potential pitfalls. It's also important to prepare a detailed campaign timeline, including launch times, updates, and various communication phases.

Creating Engaging Content: The campaign's content, especially the video and narrative material, is essential for attracting and engaging supporters. Developing a compelling and authentic story, accompanied by images, graphics, and other visual materials, is crucial for effectively communicating the value and importance of your project.

Effective Communication: Using social media and other digital platforms to promote the campaign is crucial. Creating regular and engaging communication with your audience helps build trust and interest around your project. Including regular campaign updates keeps supporters involved and informed.

Offering Attractive Rewards: Rewards for supporters must be carefully considered and designed to reflect different contribution levels. Creative and personalized rewards can increase interest and participation in your campaign. It's important to ensure that rewards are achievable, and that you can deliver them efficiently.

Post-Campaign Management: After the campaign ends, it's essential to follow through and keep the promises made. This includes thanking supporters, delivering rewards promptly, and transparently using the funds raised.

Evaluation and Learning: Finally, analyzing the campaign's success and reflecting on areas for improvement is crucial for future development. Gathering feedback from supporters and analyzing campaign data can provide valuable insights for future initiatives.

Through this detailed guide, content creators can develop a well-structured and targeted crowdfunding campaign, significantly increasing the chances of reaching and surpassing their goals.

VISION, MISSION, AND VALUE PROPOSITION

Creating an effective crowdfunding campaign requires careful consideration of three crucial components: vision, mission, and value proposition. These elements are the heart of your narrative and play a key role in communicating the value and uniqueness of your project to potential supporters.

Vision

Vision is your long-term aspiration, the big dream you are pursuing through your project. It is the image of the future you want to help bring about and should be a source of inspiration and motivation for both you and your supporters. To effectively express your vision:

- Reflect on the changes or impacts you want to see in the world as a result of your project.

- Think about how your work can contribute to a larger cause, industry, or community.

- Use evocative language to paint a clear picture of the future you are trying to create.

For example, if your project involves creating an environmental documentary, your vision might be a world where people are more aware and actively engaged in environmental conservation.

Mission

Mission describes more practically and tangibly what you do to achieve your vision. It is a statement of intent that explains your purpose and the methods you intend to use. To articulate your mission:

- Be specific about the actions you will take to move closer to your vision.

- Describe the audience or community you intend to serve.

- Explain why your work is important and how it contributes to a larger goal.

In the example of the documentary, the mission could be to produce cinematic content that educates the audience about environmental issues and promotes sustainable solutions.

Value Proposition

The value proposition is what makes your project unique and worthy of support. It is the reason why people should be interested in and contribute to your project. Consider the following aspects:

- Identify what sets your project or art apart from others in your field.

- Reflect on what you can offer supporters that they cannot get elsewhere.

- Be clear about how supporters' contributions will make a significant difference in your work.

For the environmental documentary, the value proposition could include exclusive access to behind-the-scenes footage, discussions with environmental experts, or an active role in choosing the topics covered.

Incorporating these three components into your crowdfunding campaign not only provides a clear structure and focus for your message but also helps potential supporters understand the value of their contribution and the role they can play in realizing your vision. A well-thought-out approach at this stage can make a significant difference in the success of your campaign.

DEVELOPING A CLEAR VISION AND MISSION

Developing a clear vision and mission is crucial for the success of a crowdfunding campaign as it provides guidance and direction for the project. A well-defined vision and a clear mission not only help effectively communicate with potential supporters but also provide a solid foundation for all future decisions and actions of the project.

Developing a Clear Vision

Vision is an aspirational statement that describes the long-term impact you want your project to have. It is the ideal framework you paint for the future, guided by your work and commitment. Here's how you can develop an effective vision:

- Reflect on what motivates you and what you are truly passionate about. Ask yourself why your project is important and what it hopes to change or influence.

- Think big. A vision should be bold and inspirational, something that captures attention and generates excitement.

- Be specific about how your project can influence the world, your community, or your industry. For example, if you're working on an educational project, your vision could be about transforming the landscape of education for future generations.

Articulating a Clear Mission

Mission is a concrete statement of what you do, how you do it, and why it's important. While vision is the "what," mission is the "how." The mission provides a clear path to realizing the vision. To define your mission:

- Focus on action. Your mission should describe what you do every day to move closer to your vision.

- Be clear and concise. A good mission statement is brief, to the point, and easily understandable.

- Include your audience or beneficiaries of your project. Who will you help or influence with your work? What impact will it have on them?

For example, the mission of a public art project could be to revitalize neglected urban spaces through artistic installations that engage and inspire the local community.

Aligning Vision and Mission with Your Audience

Once developed, it's essential to align your vision and mission with the audience you are trying to reach and engage through your crowdfunding project. This means communicating in a way that resonates with their values and interests. The vision and mission should be integrated into all communications, from the project website to social media to promotional materials. This helps build a consistent brand and narrative that captures the imagination of potential supporters and motivates them to actively participate in your project.

BUILDING A COMPELLING VALUE PROPOSITION

Creating a compelling value proposition is one of the most critical aspects of the successful crowdfunding campaign creation process. An effective value proposition not only grabs attention but also clearly explains to potential supporters why they should invest in your project. Here's how to develop a value proposition that resonates with your audience and motivates them to take action.

Identify What Makes Your Project Unique

Start by analyzing what sets your project or art apart. It could be an innovative approach, a unique perspective, a new solution to an existing problem, or a creative way to engage the community. Reflect on what you offer that can't be found elsewhere. This unique element is at the core of your value proposition.

Understand and Speak to Your Audience

Knowing your audience is crucial. What are their interests, needs, or problems that your project can solve or respond to? Customize your value proposition to resonate with your specific target. For example, if your project is an educational podcast, your value proposition could focus on offering unique and accessible insights in a specific field of study.

Articulate Tangible Benefits

Instead of just focusing on what the project is, explain what it will do for your supporters. This may include access to exclusive content, the opportunity to directly influence future content, or participation in a unique experience. Show how supporters' backing will lead to real and tangible benefits.

Demonstrate Credibility and Trust

Build trust by demonstrating your credibility and experience. Share your qualifications, past experiences, successes, or recognitions. If you already have a following or have received positive feedback for your work, include them in your proposition.

Create an Engaging Story

People are drawn to stories. Tell the story behind your project: its origin, your motivations, and what it hopes to achieve. Engaging storytelling can make your value proposition more memorable and personal.

Incorporate Testimonials and Social Proof

Testimonials from previous supporters or influential figures in your industry can add weight to your value proposition. Social proof can act as a powerful persuasion tool, showing potential supporters that your project is worth their commitment and support.

Be Clear and Concise

An effective value proposition should be clear, direct, and easily understandable. Avoid jargon and technical terminology that may confuse or alienate your audience.

Add a Visual Element

A visual element or an eye-catching presentation can enhance the impact of your value proposition. Whether it's graphics, photos, or videos, visual support can help communicate your idea more effectively.

Call to Action

Conclude your value proposition with a clear call to action. What do you want your potential supporters to do after reading your proposition? Be specific, whether it's signing up, donating, or simply sharing the project with others.

Remember, your value proposition is not just a list of what you offer; it's an invitation to join you on an exciting and meaningful journey. A well-developed proposition can make a difference in engaging and converting visitors into loyal supporters.

DESIGNING REWARD TIERS AND REWARDS

Effectively designing reward tiers and rewards in a crowdfunding campaign, especially on platforms like Patreon, requires careful consideration. The goal is to offer supporters contribution options that are enticing and valuable while also encouraging financial support for your project. Here are some steps and ideas to help you structure the tiers and rewards of your campaign.

1. Analyze Your Audience:

- Before defining the tiers and rewards, it's essential to understand who your potential supporters are and what might motivate them to contribute. Consider their interests, age group, spending power, and what might be valuable to them.

2. Structure Contribution Tiers:

- Create different contribution tiers to accommodate supporters with varying capacities and willingness to spend.

- Each tier should offer a reward that increases in value and exclusivity compared to the previous tier.

- Ensure that even the lower tiers offer something of value. Even a small contribution is a sign of support that should be acknowledged.

3. Reward Ideas:

- **Exclusive Content**: Offer early access or exclusive content such as blog posts, videos, podcasts, or Q&A sessions.

- **Custom Merchandise**: Create items like T-shirts, stickers, or posters related to your project.

- **Unique Experiences**: Provide experiences like virtual meetings, online workshops, or the opportunity to participate in the creative process.

- **Public Acknowledgment:** Include supporters' names in the credits of your works or publicly thank them on social media.

- **Role in Content Creation**: Give supporters the opportunity to suggest themes or content for your future works.

- **Artwork or Original Creations**: If you're an artist or creator, you can offer original artwork, signed copies, or custom commissions.

4. Clear Communication:

- Be transparent about what each contribution tier entails and when supporters can expect to receive their rewards.

- Provide clear details on how and when rewards will be delivered.

5. Managing Expectations:

- Ensure that you can manage and fulfill all the rewards you offer. Consider the time, costs, and logistics required to produce and deliver rewards.

- Prepare a plan to handle communications and supporters' questions regarding rewards.

6. Flexibility and Adaptability:

- Be open to adjusting your tiers and rewards based on feedback and interest shown by supporters.

- Monitor the success of each tier and consider adding or modifying rewards to increase the attractiveness of your campaign.

Remember, the heart of a successful crowdfunding campaign is to create a sense of community and belonging between you and your supporters. The rewards you offer should reflect your appreciation for their support and strengthen the connection with your project.

IDEATION OF EFFECTIVE FUNDING LEVELS

Coming up with effective funding levels in a crowdfunding campaign is a crucial aspect of its success. These levels should be designed to attract a wide range of supporters while offering appealing and sustainable rewards. Here's how to develop funding levels that meet both your needs and those of your supporters.

Understanding the Target Audience:

Before defining funding levels, it's essential to understand who your potential supporters are. Consider their interest in your project, their financial capacity, and what might motivate them to support you. This understanding will help you create funding levels that resonate with your audience.

Diversification of Funding Levels:

- Offer a variety of contribution levels to accommodate supporters with different budgets. Start with an accessible entry-level that anyone can afford and gradually increase the required amount.

- Ensure that even the lower levels offer value. Even a small contribution is a sign of support and commitment to your project.

- Consider including a "symbolic" level that allows people to contribute a minimal amount while still making them feel part of the project.

Defining Rewards:

- Each contribution level should offer a reward that corresponds to the value of the contribution. Rewards can range from public acknowledgments to exclusive products, unique experiences, or access to special content.

- Be creative with rewards but also realistic in your ability to deliver them. Consider the cost and logistics of producing and shipping rewards.

- For higher contribution levels, you can offer more personalized experiences, such as virtual meetings, workshops, or even the opportunity to directly influence certain aspects of your project.

Clear and Transparent Communication:

- Each funding level should be described clearly and in detail. Explain what supporters will receive and when they can expect to receive their rewards.

- Provide clear information on how the funds raised will be used. This increases trust and credibility in your project.

Feedback and Adaptability:

- After the campaign launch, monitor supporters' responses to the different funding levels. Be prepared to make changes if some levels don't attract the expected interest.

- Consider adding new levels or modifying rewards based on supporter feedback to maintain interest and engagement over time.

Remember that the primary goal of funding levels is to provide supporters with flexible and appealing options to contribute to your project while ensuring that you can support and fulfill the promises made. A well-thought-out approach to funding levels can significantly enhance the effectiveness of your crowdfunding campaign.

DEVELOPING APPEALING REWARDS FOR SUPPORTERS

Developing appealing rewards for supporters is a crucial element for the success of a crowdfunding campaign. Rewards not only incentivize financial contributions but can also help build a deeper relationship between creators and their community. Here are some strategies for creating rewards that are enticing and meaningful to your supporters.

Understanding Your Audience:

Start by identifying who your potential supporters are and what might interest them. Different groups of people may be attracted to different types of rewards. For example, fans of a podcast may appreciate access to bonus episodes, while supporters of an art project may be more interested in original artworks or limited editions.

Types of Rewards:

- **Exclusive Content**: Access to material that is not available to the general public, such as blog posts, videos, behind-the-scenes sessions, or podcast episodes.

- **Physical Products**: Items like T-shirts, posters, books, or other customized items related to your project.

- **Experiences:** Virtual meetings, workshops, Q&A sessions, or even in-person meetings that offer supporters the opportunity to interact directly with you.

- **Acknowledgments**: Including supporters' names in the credits of a film or book, or offering special thanks on social media or your website.

- **Role in Content**: Giving supporters the chance to directly influence future content, such as choosing podcast episode topics or subjects for an artwork.

- **Limited Editions or Previews**: Offering supporters access to limited editions or previews of products before they are available to the general public.

Adding Value:

- Ensure that rewards offer real added value. Even smaller rewards can be meaningful if well thought out and personalized.

- Consider creating reward tiers that increase in value and exclusivity. This can encourage higher contributions.

Sustainability and Feasibility:

- It's essential to ensure that you can fulfill and deliver all promised rewards. Carefully assess the costs and logistics required to produce and ship rewards.

- Plan ahead to avoid delays or issues in delivering rewards.

Clear Communication:

- Describe each reward clearly and in detail. Supporters should know exactly what to expect for each contribution level.

- Keep supporters updated regularly on the status of rewards, especially if there are delays or changes.

Creating appealing rewards requires creativity and careful planning, but it can make a significant difference in engaging and retaining supporters. Well-designed rewards not only incentivize funding but also strengthen the bond between you and your community.

TECHNICAL AND LEGAL ASPECTS OF CROWDFUNDING

Technical Aspects in Crowdfunding:

Platform Selection: Each crowdfunding platform has unique features, fees, and a specific audience. It's essential to choose the one that best suits your project's needs, considering factors such as the type of crowdfunding offered (e.g., donation, reward, equity), platform popularity, ease of use, and fees.

Website and Social Media Preparation: Ensure that your website and social media profiles are optimized to reflect and promote your crowdfunding campaign. These will be your primary communication channels with potential supporters, so they should be compelling, informative, and up-to-date.

Marketing and Communication Tools: Plan your marketing and communication strategy for your campaign. Use various channels, such as email marketing, social media, promotional videos, and launch events. Consider using analytics tools to monitor the performance of your advertising and communication campaigns.

Management of Contributions and Rewards: Organize an efficient system for managing received contributions and delivering promised rewards. This may include software or tools for tracking contributions, as well as a logistical plan for producing and delivering rewards.

Legal Aspects in Crowdfunding:

Regulations and Compliance: Familiarize yourself with the legal regulations related to crowdfunding in your country. This includes rules on fundraising, tax declarations, and any specific restrictions related to the type of crowdfunding you intend to use.

Intellectual Property Rights: Ensure you have the necessary rights for all material you plan to use in your campaign, including text, images, music, and videos. This is crucial to avoid potential intellectual property violations.

Agreements and Terms of Service: Read and understand the terms of service of the crowdfunding platform you choose. This will help you understand your rights and responsibilities as a platform user.

Transparency and Honesty: Be transparent about how the raised funds will be used. Providing clear and accurate information to supporters not only builds trust but is also an important legal practice to follow.

Proactively addressing these technical and legal aspects can help ensure that your crowdfunding campaign is not only effective but also compliant with regulations and safe for you and your supporters.

MANAGING PATREON SETTINGS EFFECTIVELY

Effectively managing your Patreon settings is a crucial task to maximize the success of your crowdfunding campaign. Careful attention should be given to configuring your Patreon profile. This acts as your digital storefront, so it's crucial to clearly communicate who you are, what you do, and why your project deserves support. Your biography should reflect your personality and style, while the images, including profile and cover pictures, should be of high quality and visually represent your project or brand.

When structuring support tiers, it's important that each one offers clear value to supporters. You need to balance what is attractive to your audience with what is sustainable for you to offer. Rewards such as exclusive content, early access, or unique experiences can be very appealing. It's essential that rewards are related to the value of the support tier, increasing in exclusivity and appeal as supporters commit to higher levels. Also, make sure to consider the costs and logistics in delivering these rewards, especially if they include physical items like merchandise or artwork.

Communication is another pillar of Patreon management. Keeping supporters updated not only shows that their contribution is making a difference but also helps build a community around your project. This can include updates on project development, highlights, challenges, and successes. Being transparent about progress and difficulties not only builds trust but can also encourage greater engagement from supporters.

Responding to comments and messages on Patreon is crucial for establishing and maintaining a direct relationship with your supporters. This dialogue can offer valuable insights and ideas for future content or improvements to the project. Moreover, actively engaging with supporters can turn them into ambassadors for your work, further spreading the word about your project.

Finally, leverage Patreon's analytical tools to monitor the performance of your page. This will allow you to better understand which content resonates most with your supporters, which support tiers are most popular, and how you can optimize your crowdfunding strategy over time. Regular data analysis can help you make informed decisions and make strategic adjustments to keep your campaign vibrant and growing.

TAX AND LEGAL CONSIDERATIONS FOR REWARDS

In managing a crowdfunding campaign, it is crucial to pay attention to the tax and legal considerations associated with the rewards offered. This aspect can have a significant impact on both the creator and the supporters.

First and foremost, it is important to recognize that rewards can have tax implications. Depending on the country and local legislation, the value of the rewards offered may be subject to taxation. For creators, this means that the value of the rewards may need to be included as taxable income. It is essential to consult with a tax professional to understand the specific tax regulations applicable and to handle these aspects correctly in the context of your crowdfunding campaign.

Regarding supporters, receiving rewards in exchange for a contribution can sometimes be considered as a purchase of goods or services. In this case, issues related to VAT or other sales taxes may arise. Again, these regulations vary depending on the jurisdiction and the type of reward offered. It is important that creators are transparent with supporters about any additional tax obligations that may result from receiving the rewards.

Furthermore, legal issues related to intellectual property rights and licenses must be carefully examined, especially if rewards include copyrighted content such as music, artwork, or digital products. Ensuring that you have all the necessary rights to distribute these rewards is crucial to avoid legal violations.

Another legal aspect to consider is the clarity and truthfulness of promises made in relation to the rewards. Laws on deceptive advertising and consumer protection can have implications on how rewards are described and advertised. It is important to ensure that all descriptions of rewards are accurate and not misleading.

Finally, it is good practice to provide clear terms and conditions regarding the distribution of rewards, including expected delivery times and refund or replacement policies. This helps manage supporters' expectations and provides a clear legal basis for your campaign.

In conclusion, the tax and legal considerations of crowdfunding rewards are complex and vary depending on the jurisdiction. Careful management of these aspects not only helps avoid legal and tax issues but also enhances the trust and credibility of your campaign in the eyes of supporters.

PART IV: POST-LAUNCH MANAGEMENT AND GROWTH

Part IV of the book focuses on post-launch management and the growth of a crowdfunding campaign, a fundamental aspect to ensure ongoing success and sustainability of your project. After the initial launch, your attention shifts from merely achieving the funding goal to the actual realization of the project and maintaining the interest and support of your backers.

Post-Launch Management

After the initial launch, it's essential to continue communicating with your backers. This includes regular updates on the project's status, sharing any challenges or changes in plans, and demonstrating how the raised funds are being used. Transparency and honesty in this phase are crucial to maintain the trust and support of your backers.

Additionally, efficiently managing the distribution of promised rewards is important. This may require significant logistics, especially if rewards include physical items to produce and ship. Ensure you have a clear plan for managing this process to meet backers' expectations.

Growth and Development

Once the campaign is underway and the project is in progress, start thinking about how you can further grow your project and engage your community even more. This may include:

1. Expand Your Online Presence: Utilize social media, blogs, and other platforms to reach a wider audience.

2. Create New Content or Offers: Keep backers' interest high and attract new supporters with fresh content and additional offers.

3. Actively Listen to Backer Feedback: Actively listen to and incorporate feedback from backers to guide the future development of the project.

4. Consider New Campaigns or Updates: Explore the possibility of launching new campaigns to fund subsequent project phases or new initiatives.

Supporting and Growing the Community

The community that forms around your project is one of the most valuable assets. Investing time and resources to build and maintain this community is essential. This may include creating spaces where backers can interact with each other and with you, such as online groups, forums, or live events.

Lastly, measure the success of your project not only in financial terms but also in terms of impact and community growth. Consider metrics such as backer engagement, feedback received, and the overall impact of your project. Use this information to continually improve and adapt your strategy over time.

In summary, post-launch management and the growth of a

crowdfunding campaign require careful planning, effective communication, and ongoing commitment. By maintaining a strong connection with your community and remaining flexible and responsive to their needs and feedback, you can build a solid foundation for the long-term success of your project.

MARKETING AND ENGAGEMENT

Marketing and engagement are vital components in the success of a crowdfunding campaign. A well-planned marketing strategy and active engagement with your community can make a significant difference in reaching and exceeding your funding goals. Here are some key strategies to optimize marketing and engagement for your crowdfunding campaign.

Effective Marketing Strategies

Identify Your Target Audience: Understanding your target audience is the first crucial step. Consider who would be most interested and passionate about your project. This will help you personalize your communication and focus marketing efforts where they will be most effective.

Utilize Social Media: Social media is a powerful tool for reaching a broad audience. Use it to share regular updates, behind-the-scenes stories, and exclusive content. Actively engaging with your audience on social media can also increase engagement and visibility for your project.

Create Engaging Content: Content is king. Whether it's videos, blogs, graphics, or podcasts, create content that tells the story of your project in an interesting and engaging way. Quality content can grab attention and encourage sharing, thereby increasing the reach of your campaign.

Collaborations and Partnerships: Collaborating with other creators, influencers, or brands can help expand your reach. Seek partners who share a similar audience or are aligned with your mission and values.

Events and Promotions: Organizing online events or special promotions can generate excitement around your campaign. This can include webinars, live streams, Q&A sessions, contests, or time-limited offers.

Increasing Engagement

Build a Community: Aim to build more than just supporters; strive to create a community around your project. Create spaces where your supporters can interact with each other and with you, such as Facebook groups, forums, or Discord chats.

Regular and Transparent Communication: Keep your supporters updated on progress and developments. Transparency in sharing both successes and challenges can create a sense of trust and engagement.

Feedback and Interaction: Listen to and respond to feedback and questions from your supporters. Showing that you value their opinions and ideas can strengthen their connection to your project.

Success Stories and Testimonials: Share success stories and testimonials from supporters or individuals positively impacted by your project. These human stories can be highly persuasive and reinforce your project's message.

Monitor and Adapt: Use analytical tools to monitor the effectiveness of your marketing and engagement strategies. Be prepared to adapt your tactics based on what works best.

Remember, marketing and engagement are not just about promoting your project but also about building a lasting relationship with your community. A strategic and authentic approach in these areas can have a significant impact on the success of your crowdfunding campaign.

MARKETING STRATEGIES FOR BLOGS, PODCASTS, AND YOUTUBE CHANNELS

Marketing strategies for blogs, podcasts, and YouTube channels require a targeted approach tailored to the specificities of each platform. Each medium has its own peculiarities and audience, and success depends on understanding how to best engage these different user groups.

Marketing Strategies for Blogs

- **SEO Optimization**: Use Search Engine Optimization (SEO) techniques to increase the visibility of your blog in search engines. This includes using relevant keywords, creating high-quality content, and optimizing titles and descriptions.

- **Guest Blogging and Collaborations**: Writing guest posts on other blogs or inviting guest bloggers to your site can help expand your reach. This can also involve collaborating with influencers or experts in your field.

- **Social Media Promotion**: Share your posts on social media and encourage readers to do the same. Use relevant hashtags to reach a broader audience.

- **Newsletters and Email Marketing**: Create a newsletter to keep your readers updated on new posts and other updates. This can help build a community of loyal readers.

Marketing Strategies for Podcasts

- **Social Media Promotion**: Use platforms like Twitter,

Facebook, and Instagram to share episodes, teasers, or quotes from your podcast. Consider using videos or graphics to grab attention.

- **Collaborations and Guests**: Inviting popular guests or making appearances on other podcasts can help attract new listeners.

- **Podcasting Platforms**: Ensure your podcast is available on multiple platforms (such as Apple Podcasts, Spotify, Google Podcasts) to maximize your reach.

- **Community Building:** Build a community around your podcast through online forums, discussion groups, or live events.

Marketing Strategies for YouTube Channels

- **Video Optimization for Search**: Use relevant keywords in the titles, descriptions, and tags of your videos to improve their visibility on YouTube.

- **Eye-catching Thumbnails:** Create visually appealing thumbnails for your videos. This can significantly increase the click-through rate.

- **Collaborations and Challenges**: Collaborate with other YouTubers to expand your reach. Participate in or create viral challenges that can draw attention to your channel.

- **Consistency and Regularity**: Maintain a regular and consistent publishing schedule to keep your audience engaged and anticipating your next content.

For all three platforms, understanding your audience and what resonates with them is crucial. Experimenting with different types of content and marketing strategies, and using analytics to understand what works best, will help you refine your tactics and build a loyal audience over time.

COMMUNITY ENGAGEMENT ON PATREON

Community engagement on Patreon is essential for building and maintaining a lasting relationship with your supporters. An engaged community not only financially supports your work but can also provide valuable feedback, ideas, and become a powerful word-of-mouth promotion tool. Here's how you can actively engage your community on Patreon:

Regular and Transparent Communication

- Keep your supporters consistently updated. Share project developments, celebrate successes, and be honest about challenges. This type of transparency creates a sense of trust and involvement.

- Respond to comments and messages. Direct interaction with your supporters makes them feel valued and strengthens their connection to your work.

Exclusive Content and Previews

- Offer content that is exclusive to your Patreon supporters. This can include previews of upcoming work, access to behind-the-scenes content, special blog posts, or bonus podcast episodes.

- Consider hosting exclusive live streams or Q&A sessions where supporters can interact directly with you.

Involvement in Content Creation

- Seek feedback and suggestions on your projects. This can be done through surveys, posts asking for opinions, or brainstorming sessions with supporters.

- Allow supporters to vote on certain aspects of your work, such as the theme of the next video, article, or podcast episode.

Creating Community Events and Initiatives

- Organize exclusive events for supporters, such as online meetings, workshops, or group sessions.

- Create initiatives where supporters can contribute in meaningful ways, such as collaborative projects or creative contests.

Recognition of Supporters

- Publicly thank your supporters. This can be done in your videos, podcasts, social media posts, or on your website.

- Consider creating support tiers where more generous supporters receive special recognition, such as being named in the credits of your work.

Continuous Feedback and Adaptation

- Listen to your community's feedback and adjust your engagement strategy accordingly. Supporters will feel heard and appreciated when they see that their opinions have a real impact.

Engaging your community on Patreon takes time and effort, but the benefits of having a group of loyal and active supporters are invaluable. The key is to treat your supporters not only as funders but as an integral and vital part of your creative process.

CONTINUOUS DEVELOPMENT AND ANALYSIS

Continuous development and analysis are essential components for the long-term success of any project, especially in contexts like crowdfunding campaigns or creative initiatives on platforms like Patreon. These processes allow you to understand what works, what needs improvement, and how your project can evolve over time to better meet the needs and expectations of your community. Here's how you can approach continuous development and analysis:

Monitoring and Evaluation

- Use the analytical tools available on your crowdfunding platform or social media to track the performance of your project. This includes metrics such as the number of supporters, post engagement, video views, and click-through rates.

- Regularly analyze this data to identify trends, patterns, and insights. For example, which types of posts generate more engagement? On which days and times are your supporters most active?

Community Feedback

- Direct feedback from your community is invaluable. Listen to comments, reviews, and responses to surveys to understand what your supporters appreciate and what could be improved.

- Consider holding regular feedback sessions where supporters can share their thoughts and ideas in an open and welcoming environment.

Experimentation and Innovation

- Don't be afraid to experiment with new formats, content, or ideas. Experimentation can lead to surprising discoveries about what resonates with your audience.

- Evaluate the effectiveness of these experiments through data analysis and direct feedback.

Adaptation and Improvement

- Based on your analysis and feedback, make changes and adjustments to your project. This may include changes in the type of content you produce, posting frequency, marketing strategies, or reward levels.

- Remember that adaptation and evolution are ongoing processes. Your project should be dynamic and flexible to remain relevant and engaging.

Personal and Professional Growth

- In addition to monitoring the success of your project, it's important to reflect on your personal and professional development. What skills have you acquired? How has your understanding of your audience and your field grown?

- Use these reflections to guide your future development, both as a creator and as an entrepreneur.

In conclusion, continuous development and analysis are fundamental processes that allow you to stay in tune with your audience, adapt your work to their needs and preferences, and grow both personally and professionally. This holistic approach ensures that your project remains fresh, relevant, and engaging over time.

MONITORING AND OPTIMIZATION OF THE CAMPAIGN

Monitoring and optimizing a campaign, especially in the realm of crowdfunding and online projects, are essential to ensure that your efforts achieve and maintain the desired effectiveness. Here's how you can do it effectively:

Campaign Monitoring

Use of Analytical Tools: Crowdfunding platforms and social media offer a variety of analytical tools. Utilize these tools to track important metrics such as the number of supporters, funds raised, content views, click-through rates, and engagement. These data will give you a clear idea of how your campaign is performing.

Continuous Assessment: Regularly monitor your campaign, not only to track progress toward your funding goal but also to assess the quality of engagement and the audience's response to your content.

Feedback and Interactions: Pay attention to comments and feedback received from supporters and the audience. Their reactions and opinions can provide valuable insights into what is working and what could be improved.

Campaign Optimization

Data-Driven Adaptation: Use the collected data to make strategic changes to your campaign. If certain types of posts or content are generating more engagement, consider increasing their frequency. If some promotion strategies are not working as expected, rethink or replace them.

Content Improvement: Ensure that your content is always fresh, relevant, and engaging. Adjust your content plan based on feedback and audience preferences.

Optimization of Support Levels: If you are using a platform like Patreon, periodically evaluate the effectiveness of your support levels. Be ready to modify rewards or introduce new levels if it can increase interest and support.

Seize Marketing Opportunities: Continue to seek new marketing opportunities to promote your campaign. This may include collaborations, participation in events, social media campaigns, or even offline marketing strategies.

A/B Testing: Consider conducting A/B tests on various aspects of your campaign, such as email subject lines, post images, or different calls to action. This can help you identify which elements resonate better with your audience.

In summary, continuous monitoring and optimization are essential to keep your crowdfunding campaign on the right track and maximize its success. Being proactive in evaluating and adapting your strategy will allow you to effectively respond to the needs and preferences of your audience, increasing the chances of achieving and exceeding your goals.

INNOVATIONS IN SPECIAL OFFERS AND MERCHANDISING

Innovating in special offers and merchandising can be a powerful tool to increase engagement and support for your crowdfunding campaign or on your Patreon channel. These strategies not only provide added value to your supporters but can also enhance the visibility and appeal of your project. Here are some innovative ideas in this regard:

Customized Special Offers

- Create special offers that reflect significant events, anniversaries, or holidays. For example, a special offer for your project's birthday or in conjunction with a relevant holiday.

- Offer limited-time packages that combine various products or experiences at an advantageous price.

- Implement "early bird" offers to reward the first supporters of a new initiative or a new support level.

Innovative Merchandising

- Develop merchandising that is unique to your brand or project. This can include clothing, accessories, artwork, or collectibles that are not easily found elsewhere.

- Consider using innovative production techniques or eco-friendly materials to make your merchandising more attractive and in line with your audience's values.

- Customize merchandising, allowing supporters to add a personal touch, such as their own name or a personalized message.

Exclusive Experiences

- Offer experiences that supporters cannot obtain elsewhere. This may include behind-the-scenes access, personal meetings (virtual or physical) with you or project team members, or the opportunity to participate in content creation.

- Organize special events, such as online workshops, seminars, or brainstorming sessions, where supporters can learn something new or contribute directly to your project.

Limited Editions and Collectibles

- Create limited editions of products or content that are available only for a limited time or in a limited quantity. This can create a sense of urgency and exclusivity.

- Offer collectible items that may increase in value over time, particularly appealing to collectors or the most passionate fans.

Themed Subscription Packages

- Create themed subscription packages that offer a variety of products and content related to a specific theme. This can be particularly effective if the theme resonates with your audience's interests or passions.

By incorporating these innovative ideas into your special offers and merchandising strategies, you can not only generate additional interest and excitement around your project but also create new opportunities to engage and appreciate your supporters. Remember, the key is to offer value in ways that are both authentic and aligned with the mission and identity of your project.

PART V: ADDITIONAL RESOURCES

Part V of the book is dedicated to additional resources that can support and enrich your crowdfunding campaign or your project on Patreon. These resources can range from technological tools to practical advice and can be helpful in optimizing your strategy, effectively managing the project, and deepening your understanding of crowdfunding and audience engagement. Here are some of the resources you may consider:

Technological Tools and Platforms

- Explore digital tools that can assist you in project management, such as task management software, email marketing platforms, and social media analytics tools.

- Consider using platforms for content creation, such as video or audio editing software, graphic design tools, and blog or podcast hosting services.

Training and Education

- Seek out online courses, webinars, and tutorials covering topics like digital marketing, content creation, and creative project management.

- Attend workshops or networking events to learn from industry professionals and establish valuable contacts.

Online Communities and Forums

- Join online groups and forums where other content creators and crowdfunding professionals share experiences, advice, and support. These can be found on platforms like Reddit, LinkedIn, or specific groups on Facebook.

Books and Guides

- Read books or guides that delve into crowdfunding, digital marketing, storytelling, and brand development. These can offer insights and strategies that may not be immediately apparent.

Professional Consulting

- Consider consulting with experts or consultants in specific areas such as marketing, financial management, or legal aspects. This can be especially useful if you are venturing into unfamiliar territory or if your project reaches a scale that requires more sophisticated management.

Feedback and Case Studies

- Analyze case studies of successful crowdfunding campaigns or those similar to your project. Learning from real examples can provide practical insights and inspiration.

- Utilize surveys and feedback tools to better understand the needs and desires of your audience.

Incorporating these resources into your project will not only help you better manage your campaign and optimize your approach but will also provide you with a broader foundation of knowledge and skills that you can apply in future initiatives. Remember, the world of crowdfunding and content creation is continually evolving, so staying informed and open to learning is crucial.

CASE STUDIES AND ANALYSIS

In a world where crowdfunding has become a vital bridge between creativity and realizing dreams, the stories of Alessia, Marco, and Elisa shine as vivid examples of diverse trajectories in the journey of crowdfunding.

Alessia's Story, the Innovative Artist

Alessia, a visual artist from Rome, had a bold idea: to create a series of interactive art installations that explored the nuances of contemporary Italian culture. Launching her campaign on Kickstarter, she shared not only the artistic concept but also her personal story and passion for art. Her videos, filled with evocative images of her previous works, captured the attention of a wide audience. However, what truly solidified her success was her ability to tell a story that resonated on a personal level with her supporters, offering them the opportunity to be part of something unique and culturally significant.

Marco's Journey, the Educational Podcaster

Marco, an educator from Turin with a passion for history, launched a podcast that told lesser-known stories of Italian history. When he decided to expand his project through Patreon, he adopted a direct engagement approach with his audience. Every week, he proposed themes and accepted suggestions for upcoming episodes. This ongoing interaction created a close-knit and engaged community where supporters felt heard and valued. The key to Marco's success was his ability to transform his listeners from mere listeners into active participants in the creative process.

Elisa's Lesson, the Fashion Creator

Elisa, a young fashion designer from Milan, experienced a different story. After launching an exciting campaign on Indiegogo for a new sustainable clothing line, she encountered challenges in keeping up with the promised delivery schedule. Despite the initial high interest, her lack of regular updates and poor communication gradually eroded the trust of her supporters. This experience taught Elisa an important lesson about managing expectations and the importance of transparency in crowdfunding campaigns. After acknowledging these mistakes, she worked to rebuild trust with her supporter base, promising greater openness and regularity in updates.

These stories illustrate different facets of crowdfunding. While Alessia and Marco found success through emotional storytelling and community engagement, Elisa's story serves as a critical reminder of the importance of effective management and communication. Together, they represent a mosaic of lessons and inspirations for anyone venturing into the world of crowdfunding.

EXAMPLES OF SUCCESS ON VARIOUS CROWDFUNDING PLATFORMS

Let's imagine the stories of three individuals, each of whom has found success in different ways on different crowdfunding platforms, reflecting the variety and dynamism of this space.

The Story of Luke, the Innovative Musician on Patreon

Luke is a musician from Florence who found a unique niche for his talent on Patreon. He began creating musical compositions that blend traditional Italian elements with modern influences. Through Patreon, he offered his supporters exclusive access to live online performances, personalized music lessons, and the ability to influence his upcoming compositions. The key to his success was his ability to create a true community around his music, where supporters felt involved in the creative process.

Sofia's Success, the Content Creator on Kickstarter

Sofia, a documentarian from Milan, used Kickstarter to fund an ambitious project: a documentary about the history of lesser-known Italian cities. Through a well-designed campaign, she shared her vision and the story behind the project, attracting the attention of history and Italian culture enthusiasts. Her success on Kickstarter was amplified by sharing exclusive clips and behind-the-scenes glimpses of the production process, creating a strong bond with her backers.

John and His Travel Blog on Indiegogo

John is a travel blogger from Naples who launched a campaign on Indiegogo to fund an undiscovered tour of lesser-known regions in Italy. By offering personalized merchandise to supporters, such as travel guides and illustrated maps, and providing regular updates with stories and photos, John created an engaging campaign that captured the imagination of those who love to explore hidden places. His ability to tell compelling stories and offer tangible rewards made his Indiegogo campaign a notable success.

These examples demonstrate how crowdfunding can be a powerful means to bring creative and innovative projects to life. Whether it's music, filmMaking, or travel, platforms like Patreon, Kickstarter, and Indiegogo offer individuals the opportunity to bring their ideas to the public and find supporters who share their passion.

IN-DEPTH ANALYSIS OF SUCCESSFUL PATREON CAMPAIGNS

Immersed in the historic alleys of Genoa, Adriano, a talented illustrator and graphic artist, has found a stage for expressing his art on Patreon. His series of comics, an intriguing blend of mythology and modern themes, has captured the interest of a vast international community. Adriano has transformed his Patreon account into a virtual gallery, where supporters can access exclusive content such as sketches, creative processes, and preview episodes. His monthly Q&A sessions, where fans can engage in in-depth discussions about characters and plots, have created an ongoing dialogue between him and his supporters, making each new release a community event.

In the bustling heart of Bologna, Caterina, a passionate music history podcaster, has skillfully woven compelling narratives around overlooked musical figures. Her podcast "Hidden Notes" delves into the stories of lesser-known composers, enriching each episode with exclusive interviews and detailed analysis. On Patreon, Caterina offers her listeners a richer experience: special episodes, post-episode discussions, and even virtual meetings with experts and musicians. Her platform has become a meeting point for a niche of enthusiasts, creating a sense of belonging and cultural exchange.

In Turin, Martina's story is one of transformation: from a

chef and food blogger to an innovator in the crowdfunding world. Her culinary journey on Patreon has evolved into a unique experience for her supporters. She offers exclusive recipes, cooking video tutorials, and in-depth guides on ingredients and culinary techniques. Her culinary book club is an absolute novelty: every month, supporters cook together a dish selected by Martina and discuss it in a virtual evening, combining a love for reading with a passion for cooking. Martina has created a warm and welcoming corner in the vast online world, where food becomes a vehicle for stories, traditions, and encounters.

These three stories — Adriano, Caterina, and Martina — not only demonstrate the versatility of Patreon as a crowdfunding platform but also emphasize the importance of community engagement. Through their work, they have created unique spaces for dialogue, learning, and sharing passions, demonstrating that success on Patreon goes beyond mere funding. It's about building bridges, sharing experiences, and nurturing a community around shared interests and passions.

FREQUENTLY ASKED QUESTIONS AND USEFUL TOOLS

How to Choose the Right Crowdfunding Platform for My Project?

Selecting the most suitable crowdfunding platform is crucial and should be based on several key factors. First, consider the nature of your project and your target audience. Platforms like Kickstarter and Indiegogo are ideal for innovative, creative, and product-oriented projects due to their extensive user base and visibility. If your project requires ongoing support and focuses on artistic or creative content such as videos, podcasts, or blogs, Patreon might be more suitable. Here, supporters commit to regular contributions, creating a more stable income stream.

Also, analyze the funding structures of different platforms. Kickstarter follows an "all-or-nothing" approach, meaning you must reach your funding goal within a certain period to receive the funds. Indiegogo offers greater flexibility with the option to keep the funds raised even if you don't reach the full goal. Consider these aspects based on your strategy and risk tolerance.

Another crucial factor is the fee system of each platform. Carefully examine how much it will cost to use the service, including any hidden fees or additional charges, and how this will impact your overall budget.

Evaluate the customization options and features of each platform as well. The ability to personalize your crowdfunding page, effectively communicate with supporters, and offer attractive rewards can make a significant difference in engaging your audience.

Finally, consider the reputation and success stories of the platform. Examine the stories of other projects similar to yours and assess their experience on the platform. This can give you an idea of the likelihood of success for your project.

How to Set the Funding Goal?

Setting the funding goal requires an accurate assessment of your financial needs. This includes production costs, marketing, shipping, and platform fees. It's also important to consider a margin for unexpected expenses. Ensure that the goal is realistic and achievable, based on an accurate estimate of costs and an understanding of your target audience.

How to Create a Compelling Campaign Message?

An effective message should tell the story of your project, why it's important, and what makes it unique. Focus on how your project can emotionally resonate with potential supporters. Use images, videos, and persuasive storytelling to create a connection with your audience. Being transparent about goals, fund usage, and rewards also helps build trust.

What Are Best Practices for Managing Rewards?

Effectively managing rewards is crucial to keeping supporters satisfied and engaged. Choose rewards that are desirable for your supporters but sustainable for you to produce and deliver. Be clear about delivery timing and communicate any delays or changes. It's also helpful to consider digital reward options, which can reduce costs and logistical complexity.

How Can I Maximize Campaign Visibility?

To maximize visibility, use a combination of social media, public relations, email marketing, and networking. Create engaging and shareable content that supporters can spread within their networks. Collaborating with influencers or other creators can also help reach a broader audience. Don't underestimate the power of word-of-mouth.

What Are Effective Strategies for Maintaining Engagement After the Campaign?

After the campaign ends, continue engaging supporters with regular updates on the project's status. Consider offering exclusive or behind-the-scenes content to keep interest high. Listening to and responding to supporter feedback is also crucial for building a lasting community.

By incorporating these frequently asked questions and using the right tools, you'll be well-equipped to navigate the world of crowdfunding and optimize the chances of success for your campaign.

What Are Useful Tools for Managing a Crowdfunding Campaign?

Project Management Tools

Trello or Asana: These project management tools are ideal for organizing tasks, deadlines, and team collaborations. They allow you to track the progress of the campaign and stay on course with your goals.

Google Workspace: This package offers tools like Docs, Sheets, and Calendar, useful for creating and sharing content, planning activities, and organizing meetings.

Email Marketing Tools

Mailchimp: Perfect for creating and sending newsletters and updates to supporters. It also provides detailed analytics on your email performance.

Sendinblue: Another excellent option for email campaigns, with additional features for marketing automation.

Creative Editing Software

Adobe Creative Suite: Includes Photoshop, Illustrator, and InDesign, essential tools for creating professional images and graphics for your campaign.

Final Cut Pro or Adobe Premiere Pro: Video editing software to create high-quality videos useful for presenting your project or providing regular updates to supporters.

Analytics and Social Media Tools

Google Analytics: Essential for tracking traffic to your

crowdfunding page and understanding where your visitors are coming from.

Hootsuite or Buffer: These tools allow you to schedule and monitor social media posts, providing valuable analytics to understand which content works best.

Other Useful Tools

Canva: A fantastic resource for non-designers. It offers easy-to-use design templates and tools to create eye-catching images for your campaign.

Zoom or Skype: To organize virtual meetings with your team or for live sessions with supporters.

By using these tools, you can optimize the management of your crowdfunding campaign, from planning to promotion, monitoring, and analyzing its success.

CREATING A SUPPORT GROUP FOR CREATORS

Developing an Engagement Strategy

In addition to conveying your vision, it's crucial to develop an engagement strategy for your support group. Define how you will interact with members, what key points of contact will be, and how you'll keep their interest in the project high. This may include regular updates, online discussions, events, or awareness-raising activities.

Building Strong Relationships

Your support group should not just be a collection of people helping you raise funds. It should be a community of individuals who share a passion for your project. Invest time in building strong relationships with group members by sharing your experiences, listening to their ideas, and showing gratitude for their support.

Utilizing Group Resources

Apart from emotional support and project promotion, your support group may have specific skills and resources that can be used to enhance crowdfunding. For instance, they might be able to provide graphic design, marketing, or legal consulting services. Leverage these resources to improve your campaign and increase the chances of success.

Involving the Group in Planning

Including your support group in crowdfunding planning can be a significant step. Seek their feedback on fundraising strategies, supporter rewards, and promotion tactics. They can offer valuable insights and creative ideas to make your campaign more appealing.

Recognition and Gratitude

Lastly, it's essential to recognize and show gratitude to members of your support group. Show them how important they are to the project's success, perhaps by including them in credits or offering exclusive benefits. Sincere recognition can strengthen the bond between you and your supporters.

Monitoring and Adaptation

Crowdfunding is a dynamic process, and it's important to continually monitor the campaign's progress and adapt the strategy based on results. Involve your support group in this evaluation and adaptation process, seeking their input on how to improve performance and achieve funding goals.

Creating a solid support group and engaging with it effectively can make the difference between success and failure in crowdfunding. Be sure to plan carefully and invest time and energy in managing this valuable resource for your project.

SHARING IDEAS AND BEST PRACTICES

In the dynamic world of crowdfunding, sharing ideas and adopting best practices play a fundamental role in shaping the success of creators and innovators. This chapter will explore in detail how collaboration, open discussion, and shared learning are the very essence of crowdfunding, tangibly influencing the growth and improvement of crowdfunding campaigns.

The Crowdfunding Community: An Invaluable Resource

Crowdfunding is more than just a fundraising platform. It's a global community of creative minds, a place where creators from all sectors and disciplines come together to share their visions and seek community support. This community is the beating heart of idea sharing and best practices in crowdfunding. Here, creators share their experiences, explore common challenges, and inspire each other.

Dialogue Among Creators: An Inexhaustible Source of Inspiration

Online forums, social media chats, and discussion platforms are the virtual spaces where creator dialogues come to life. These channels are authentic digital town squares where creators can share their stories, seek advice, and learn from others. Conversations are fueled by contagious energy, where shared experiences often lead to creative solutions for common challenges. Here, creators from every corner of the world meet, challenge, and support each other, creating an ecosystem of continuous learning.

The Importance of Feedback: A Guide to Refinement

In the crowdfunding process, feedback is a precious treasure to gather. Receiving input from other creators or supporters can be key to refining project presentations, revising reward offerings, and fine-tuning promotional strategies. Creators who listen and adapt based on constructive feedback often find the right path to success. Open and honest sharing of encountered challenges is what makes this improvement process so powerful.

Collaboration Among Creators: Unified Backgrounds and Skills

One of the most powerful forms of idea sharing is collaboration among creators. When two or more creators join forces on similar or complementary projects, unique synergies are created. Resources, skills, and knowledge merge to achieve better results than each could achieve alone. This collaborative spirit can lead to successful partnerships and shared projects that attract a wider audience, demonstrating how powerful resource sharing is in the world of crowdfunding.

Online Resources: A Virtual Library

In addition to interpersonal relationships, the online world offers a wide range of resources dedicated to sharing ideas and best practices in crowdfunding. Blogs, webinars, podcasts, and practical guides provide detailed advice on how to optimize a crowdfunding campaign, including marketing strategies, effective communication, and post-campaign management. These resources are like a virtual library, ready to be consulted by creators seeking inspiration and guidance.

Continuous Learning: An Imperative

In the world of crowdfunding, there is no magic formula for success, as platforms, trends, and supporter preferences can change rapidly. Therefore, the sharing of ideas and best practices is an ongoing process. Successful creators are those who remain open to continuous learning, constantly adapting their strategies based on shared experiences and knowledge within the crowdfunding community. The willingness to learn and grow is an attribute that distinguishes successful creators.

In conclusion, sharing ideas and best practices are the heart and soul of crowdfunding. Creators who embrace this collaborative spirit often achieve more rewarding results and build lasting relationships with their supporter community. Sharing knowledge is a crucial path to success in the ever-changing world of crowdfunding, where creativity and collaboration come together to bring successful projects to life.

CONCLUSION

Summary and Next Steps

In this chapter dedicated to sharing ideas and best practices in crowdfunding, we have explored the crucial role that collaboration and shared learning play in determining the success of projects and ideas. We have seen how the crowdfunding community is a valuable opportunity for creators to connect, share experiences, and refine their strategies.

Summary of Key Themes

- We began by recognizing the intrinsic value of the crowdfunding community as a source of inspiration, support, and mutual learning.

- We examined the dialogue among creators as one of the main drivers of idea sharing and best practices, highlighting the importance of online forums, social media, and discussion platforms.

- We emphasized the importance of feedback as a tool for refining crowdfunding campaigns and adapting to the needs of supporters.

- We explored the powerful dynamics of collaboration among creators, where resources, skills, and knowledge merge to achieve extraordinary results.

- We mentioned the rich online resources available to creators, such as blogs, webinars, podcasts, and practical guides, which offer detailed advice on how to optimize every aspect of crowdfunding.

- Finally, we underscored the importance of continuous learning as an imperative in the ever-evolving world of crowdfunding.

Next Steps

As we conclude this section, it's important to remember that sharing ideas and best practices in crowdfunding is an ongoing process with no limits. Every creator is encouraged to continue actively participating in the community, seeking inspiration, providing feedback, and collaborating with other innovators. This collaborative spirit not only enhances one's own project but also contributes to the overall growth of the crowdfunding community.

Furthermore, it's crucial to remain flexible and ready to adapt strategies based on new knowledge and emerging trends. Crowdfunding is an ever-evolving environment, and successful creators are those who can adapt to the challenges and opportunities that arise along the way.

Lastly, we invite all creators to continue exploring online resources and actively participating in forums and discussions on their chosen crowdfunding platform. This is one of the most effective ways to stay updated on best practices and to build meaningful connections with other creators and supporters.

In conclusion, sharing ideas and best practices is the beating heart of the crowdfunding community. By sharing their knowledge and learning from others, creators can overcome obstacles, achieve goals, and create successful projects. Collaboration continues to be the key to progress and the promising future of crowdfunding.

SUMMARY OF KEY POINTS

In our exploration of crowdfunding for digital creators, we have addressed several fundamental aspects that are essential for success in this ever-evolving world. Here is a summary of the key points covered in the book:

Part I: Fundamentals of Crowdfunding

Why Crowdfunding Is Effective: We have examined the multiple benefits that crowdfunding offers to digital creators, from funding their passions to active engagement with a community of supporters.

Types of Crowdfunding: We have explored the various crowdfunding modalities, including Donation, Lending, Reward, Equity, and Content Crowdfunding, helping you select the model that best suits your needs.

Part II: Crowdfunding for Content Creators

Specific Strategies for Different Platforms: We have explored unique approaches for blogs, podcasts, and YouTube channels, highlighting how Patreon can serve as a versatile tool for monetizing your content.

Setting Up a Successful Campaign on Patreon: We have analyzed the unique features of Patreon and guided you in creating and customizing an effective campaign on this platform.

Part III: Building Your Campaign

Vision, Mission, and Value Proposition: We have assisted you in developing a clear vision and mission and in constructing a compelling value proposition for your supporters.

Designing Funding Levels and Rewards: We have examined how to devise effective funding levels and develop attractive rewards for your supporters.

Technical and Legal Aspects: We have provided information on Patreon settings and tax and legal considerations for rewards.

Part IV: Post-Launch Management and Growth

Marketing and Engagement: We have addressed marketing strategies for blogs, podcasts, and YouTube channels, as well as community engagement on Patreon.

Continuous Development and Analysis: We have shown you how to monitor and optimize your campaign over time, as well as how to innovate with special offers and merchandising.

Part V: Additional Resources

Case Studies and Analysis: We have presented successful examples on various platforms and analyzed successful Patreon campaigns in detail.

Frequently Asked Questions and Useful Tools: We have answered common questions and provided a list of useful tools to assist you in your crowdfunding campaign.

In conclusion, we have thoroughly explored crowdfunding for digital creators, providing a comprehensive guide that will enable you to embark on your journey into the world of collective funding with confidence and success. Remain open to continuous learning, sharing of ideas, and best practices, and remember that crowdfunding is a dynamic journey that requires adaptability and constant commitment. With the right approach, you can create a lasting impact and build a strong base of supporters for your creative projects.

STRATEGIES FOR SUSTAINING SUCCESS OVER TIME

At the end of this journey through the world of crowdfunding for digital creators, we find ourselves at a crossroads. You have learned the techniques, strategies, and best practices necessary to launch a successful crowdfunding campaign. However, success is not just a destination; it is an ongoing process that requires dedication and constant care. Here are some key strategies to ensure that your crowdfunding success endures over time:

Nurture Your Relationships

The supporters you gained during your crowdfunding campaign are an invaluable resource. Continue to nurture these relationships by involving them in your creative endeavors and expressing gratitude for their ongoing support. Maintain open dialogue with your community through regular updates, discussions, and exclusive previews. These bonds can grow and flourish over time, leading to sustained support and word-of-mouth referrals from your supporters.

Continuous Innovation

The digital world is ever-evolving, and so should your crowdfunding strategies. Be open to innovation and constantly seek ways to enhance your content offerings and rewards for supporters. New formats, approaches, and tools can keep your campaign fresh and engaging over time.

Listen and Learn

The feedback from your supporters and community is a priceless treasure. Listen to what they have to say, whether it's suggestions to improve your content or new ideas for rewards and incentives. Demonstrate that you take their feedback seriously and conduct regular surveys to gather valuable insights. Continuous learning will help you keep your crowdfunding aligned with the needs and desires of your supporters.

Diversification of Income Sources

While crowdfunding may represent a significant portion of your income, you should never rely entirely on one source of funding. Seek opportunities to diversify your income sources, which could include sponsorships, merchandise sales, consulting, or collaborations. This diversification not only reduces financial risk but also allows you to explore new ways to expand your creativity.

Community and Mutual Support

Do not underestimate the power of the digital creator community. Maintain close ties with other creators and look for opportunities for collaboration and mutual support. Sharing ideas, experiences, and resources can lead to synergies that strengthen your position in the digital world.

Stay Focused on Your Mission

Always remember your mission and why you embarked on your crowdfunding journey. Keep the passion and enthusiasm that fueled your initial success alive. A deep connection with your mission will inspire both you and your supporters to continue supporting your work over time.

Ultimately, crowdfunding is an exciting and ever-evolving journey. With a combination of dedication, adaptability, and relationship-building, you can maintain and cultivate your success over time. Always remember that your community of supporters is at the heart of this journey, and their commitment and affection are the foundations upon which you can build a bright future for your creative projects.

AUTHOR'S NOTE

Patrick Labert is a passionate and experienced author in the field of crowdfunding for digital creators. With a career spanning years of experience in the world of crowdfunding and a passion for digital innovation, Patrick Labert has dedicated his time to exploring, experimenting, and sharing best practices to help creators bring their projects to life.

With his detailed guidance and deep knowledge, Patrick Labert aims to inspire and guide aspiring digital creators to success in their crowdfunding campaigns. His mission is to share his wealth of knowledge and offer valuable support to those seeking to bring their creative ideas to fruition.

Through this guide, Patrick Labert provides a comprehensive overview and practical advice on how to approach crowdfunding successfully, whether you are a blogger, podcaster, or content creator on YouTube. His words reflect a commitment to the art of funding dreams and the importance of sharing knowledge to build a successful community.

Whether you are starting your crowdfunding journey or seeking fresh perspectives, Patrick Labert will guide you with passion and dedication, providing you with the tools needed to achieve your creative goals.

Explore a World of Knowledge and Inspiration

Visit **www.libriutili.it**

Dear reader,

We hope you have found inspiration and usefulness within the pages of this book. If your thirst for knowledge and personal growth is not yet satisfied, we have a special surprise for you!

We invite you to explore the world of LuminaLibria at www.libriutili.it, where a universe of books awaits you. LuminaLibria is an oasis for every type of reader, offering a wide range of genres that will enrich your reading experience.

For Little Explorers: Browse our collection of Children's Books and Stories for Children, perfect for sparking the imagination and curiosity of the youngest readers.

For Art and Relaxation: Let yourself be captivated by our Coloring Books for Adults and Children, a creative way to relax and express yourself.

For Personal Growth: Explore our Self-Help, Personal Growth, and Biographies books to inspire and motivate you on your life journey.

For Curious Spirits: Deepen your spiritual journey with our Books on Spiritual Topics.

This is only a small part of what LuminaLibria has to offer. We believe that every book is a window to new worlds, ideas, and possibilities. Whether you are seeking adventure, knowledge, or inspiration, you will find a book that speaks to your heart at www.libriutili.it. And remember, the website features books in Italian, English, and Spanish.

Scan the QR Code below to begin your journey into the world of LuminaLibria.

Thank you for accompanying us on this journey of discovery and growth. We are excited to see you explore even more with LuminaLibria.

Happy reading and continued exploration!

The LuminaLibria Team